D1315459

ALASKA
& THE YUKON

ALASKA
& THE YUKON

Barbara Paulding Thrasher

GALLERY BOOKS
An imprint of W.H. Smith Publishers Inc.
112 Madison Avenue
New York, New York 10016

A Bison Book

Published by Gallery Books
A Division of W H Smith Publishers Inc.
112 Madison Avenue
New York, New York 10016

Produced by
Bison Books Corp.
17 Sherwood Place
Greenwich, CT 06830

Copyright © 1985 Bison Books Corp.

All rights reserved. No part of this book may be
reproduced or transmitted in any form or by any means
without written permission from the Publisher.

ISBN 0-8317-0208-7

Printed in Holland

1 2 3 4 5 6 7 8 9 10

To my parents
Acknowledgements

The author and publisher would like to thank the following people who have helped in the
reparation of this book: Richard and Sonja Glassman, who designed it; Thomas G.
Aylesworth, who edited it; Mary R. Raho, who did the photo research.

Picture credits

Marcello Bertinetti: 18-19, 22-23, 25 (bottom), 28-29, 34 (top), 34-35, 36 (top), 41 (top and
bottom), 49 (both), 54, 55 (bottom right), 59 (top).
Freelance Photographers Guild: J Brenneis (32, 33 top); E Cooper (50-51): H. Critchell (55
top right); D Davis (38-39); T Duerst (81 top); T Funk (1); K Gunnar (55 left, 56-57); D
Hall (44-45); R Harrington (70 bottom, 71, 76-77, 78-79, 84-85, 85, 90-91, 92-93, 94); P
Henschel (12-13, 60-61, 75 bottom); Hubbell (70 top); W King (46-47, 48 top and bottom);
E Manewal (23 top, 24 left and bottom right, 42, 43 top right, 65, 72 left, 72-73 bottom); R
Romei (10-11, 14 top left and bottom, 15, 24-25 top, 26, 52, 68); R Rowan (62-63); G
Rowell (2-3, 37 top, 40-41, 64); L L Rue III (37 left middle); J Schneider (43 top left); C
Smith (66-67); Tabby (20-21); B Waterman (17 top right and bottom left); W Wells (69).

Jeff Gnass: 30-31, 53 (bottom).
R J Hayes: 80.
Bill Luria: 6-7, 23 (bottom right), 27, 36 (bottom), 59 (bottom), 75 (top).
P McCloskey: 93 (bottom right).
Parks Canada: 88 (bottom), 89 (top right).
Jack Schick: 16, 81 (bottom), 82-83, 86-87, 88 (top), 89 (top left), 93 (top right), 95.
Allan Seiden: 4-5, 33 (bottom), 58-59, 72-73 (top), 73 (right), 74 (top).
Tim Thompson: 14 (top and bottom right), 17 (top left and bottom right), 37 (bottom left
and right), 43 (bottom), 74 (bottom), 89 (bottom), 96.
U.S. Geologic Survey: 8-9.
Angela Whiote: 34 (bottom), 53 (top left and right).

Contents

Introduction

The call of the wild in Alaska and the Yukon is as strong as it has ever been. This vast wilderness still contains ravines and remote mountains that no man has ever seen. Much has been written about the challenge and magnificence of this frontier—the tales of Jack London, the poems of Robert Service, the accounts of John Muir—but few capture the amazing kaleidoscope of landscape, culture and adventure that characterizes Alaska and the Yukon.

By far the largest of the United States, Alaska sprawls over 569,000 square miles in North America's extreme northwest. Bordered on the east by Canada and on all other sides by ocean, Alaska's rugged mountains, huge glaciers, scenic waterways and endless tundra comprise a land that is as varied as it is vast. Alaska has many faces—bustling ports and oil refineries, engorged rivers roaring at spring break-up, the stillness of a mountain peak in the midnight sun. It is a place unlike any other.

Russians colonized Alaska in the eighteenth century. They carried on a lively fur trade, leaving cultural and architectural landmarks that remain today. The United States bought Alaska from Russia in 1867 for $7.2 million, and the first gold discoveries less than 20 years later foreshadowed the legendary gold rushes that would follow. Alaska's native people, mainly Aleuts, Eskimos and Indians, would adjust only partially to the changes that goldseekers presaged. In 1912 Alaska became a territory, but it was the building of the Alaska Highway during World War II that helped Alaska achieve statehood in 1959.

The vast reaches of the Yukon Territory were first explored in 1842. The boom that made the Yukon a territory, though, came with the enormous gold strike near Dawson City in 1898. With a total population of about 24,500, the Yukon's 186,600 square miles are enriched by a wealth of unspoiled wilderness lands.

The great lands of Alaska and the Yukon still beckon—they are one of the world's last frontiers.

Canoers paddle in tranquil waters off Admiralty Island, one of the largest islands in southeast Alaska. Established as a National Monument in 1980, the island is 957,587 acres in area.

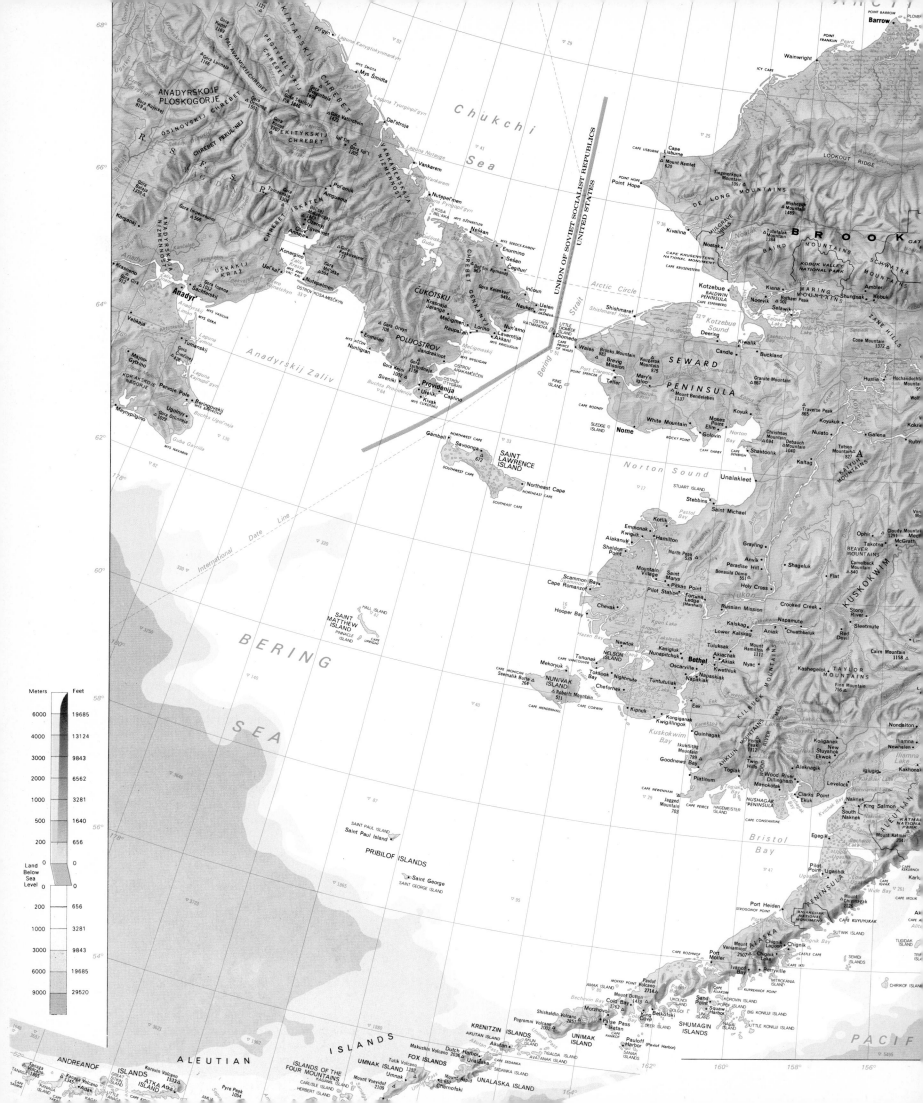

© Rand McNally & Co., R.L. 85-S-33

Southeast

Southeast

Alaska's southeast is comprised of a long, narrow and mountainous strip of land bordering Canada, and the Alexander Archipelago, an island chain of mountains that jut above the water. Carved by glaciers during the Great Ice Age a million years ago, the 500-mile-long Panhandle, as this region is called, offers a wealth of natural beauty in its national parks and monuments. Emerald-green forests of spruce and hemlock, dramatic fjords, ice-blue glaciers and jagged mountains harbor deer, porcupine, beaver, gray wolves, bald eagles, salmon, whales, porpoise and many other forms of land and marine animal life. Almost all of southeastern Alaska lies within Tongass National Forest, the largest national forest in the United States.

But this area is rich in culture as well, containing about 1000 islands and the major towns of Juneau, the state capital; Sitka, the former Russian capital; Skagway, the gold rush tent town; Haines; Petersburg; Wrangell and Ketchikan. Each settlement exudes its own particular spirit and local color. The old Russian and Indian cultures live on in churches and totem poles as well as in dance and legend. Festivals revive the days of the gold rush as well as providing contests for native sports and arenas for native arts and crafts. And the temperate climate overall makes the southeast a hospitable place to live as well as to visit.

With Skagway to the south, called 'the gateway to Alaska' because of its ferry connections, the magnificent Glacier Bay National Park to the north, the mile-and-a-half high Coast Mountains to the east, blue ocean to the west, and a virtual playground of islands and waterways between, the Panhandle is truly Alaska's greatest treasure.

Alaska cotton fills a field in early autumn with its bursting, feathery blooms. A favorite in dried floral arrangements, Alaska cotton is very common in the southeast region of Alaska.

Pages 10-11: The late afternoon sun creates a placid scene at Auke Bay, just north of Juneau at the tip of Douglas Island. Campgrounds and a ferry station make this a favorite spot.

13

Left: The stately Governor's Mansion in Juneau was built in 1912. This white-pillared colonial is located near other State buildings.
Top left: The Fourth of July celebration in Juneau, complete with parade and carnival, displays Alaska's pride in being the 49th state.
Top right: Juneau at night reflects its colorful lights in the Gastineau Channel. This bustling city is especially lively during the winter legislative session.
Above: A dramatic view through an ice cave in the Mendenhall Glacier. Located 13 miles north of Juneau, the glacier is a mile and a half wide.
Right: A dusting of snow creates a picturesque scene in downtown Juneau.

Left: The New Archangel Russian Dancers in Sitka perform traditional Russian folk dances.
Above: Local color isn't all that is featured in Juneau's Red Dog Saloon, which recalls the days when wagers were made in the form of gold dust. The honky-tonk nightlife in this landmark tavern, complete with sawdust-covered floor, includes community singing and foot stomping amidst bear trap decor.
Below: With wooden sidewalks and false-fronted buildings, Skagway displays its origins as a gold rush outpost. The Eagles Hall features 'Skaguay in the Days of 98,' a dramatic performance recreating a colorful past.

Opposite page: Native costumes add color to the Southeast Alaska State Fair in Haines. Held the third week in August, the annual fair features a parade, horse show, craft exhibits and lots of food.
Left: Many communities in the southeast have their own native dance groups that keep alive the native language and music. Here the performance features a totemic stage set and colorful clothing.

The port city of Haines nestles on a wooded peninsula at the northern end of the Lynn Canal.

A glacier calves icebergs into chilly waters.
Alaska's many glaciers were explored and
studied by the great naturalist John Muir.

Left: Established in 1925, Glacier Bay National Park is comprised of 3,280,000 acres and contains 20 tremendous glaciers, fed by the Takhinsha and Fairweather Mountain Ranges.
Above: Indian Paintbrush is just one of the many wildflowers common to Alaska's southeast. Others include bunchberry, the lovely lupine, showy fireweed and the state flower, the forget-me-not.
Below: Kayaking is one of the best ways to view the glaciers, fords, marine life and birds of Glacier Bay National Park.

Far left: Detail of a totem pole on Shakes Island in Wrangell. The Raven pictured here is a common motif in Tlingit and Haida Indian totem poles and represents a tribal subdivision.

Above: The farthest south and east of the Panhandle's major cities, bustling Ketchikan is called 'The Salmon Capitol of the World.'

Left: An Indian works on restoring a totem pole in Haines. Traditionally carved of cedar and painted black, red and blue-green, totem poles were created to commemorate significant events, honor the dead or mock an enemy.

Middle left: Overlooking scenic Tongass Narrows, Totem Bight State Historic Park in Ketchikan contains 14 totem poles and a community house.

25

Left: Saint Michael's Russian Orthodox Cathedral in Sitka is a reminder of the Russian role in this city's history. A working church and seat of the Russian Orthodox church in Alaska, this replica of the original cathedral, which was destroyed by fire, was built in 1976. The delicate spire and Byzantine dome give the church a distinctive appearance.

Above: Sawdust flies during the All-Alaska Logging Championship in Sitka. Held each year in June, the championships attract contestants from all over the state to test their skill in one of Alaska's most important industries. The roar of chainsaws and the smell of wood chips fill the air as lumberjacks move from one event to the next.

Southwest and Southcentral

Southwest and Southcentral

The southwest and southcentral region of Alaska extends west from the Chugach Mountains, which mark off the Panhandle to the east, to the Aleutian and Pribilof Islands in the extreme west. Mountainous and forested, but sprinkled with fertile valleys and areas of tundra plain, this vast region contains much more than its fair share of spectacular scenery.

The rugged coastal mountains along the Gulf of Alaska harbor an array of wildlife, scattered villages and rain forests. Prince William Sound at the western edge of the mountain range is a rainy, island-dotted area, offering panoramic views of the magnificent coastline and its own enormous Columbia Glacier. The Sound is a favorite spot for whale-watching, but its diversity of birds— including the colorful harlequin duck—make this an attraction as well. West of Prince William Sound, the Kenai Peninsula dips south into the Gulf, forming Cook Inlet to the west. The Kenai Mountains form the eastern part of the Peninsula, and plains slope to the western shore, where Kenai is located. One of the oldest settlements in Alaska, the city has its roots as a Russian trading post in 1791.

Cook Inlet, named for Captain James Cook, extends north to Anchorage, the state's largest and youngest city. With a population of more than 200,000, modern and cosmopolitan Anchorage is called 'the Big Apple' of Alaska. Southwest of Anchorage, the Alaska Peninsula and Aleutian Island Chain curve into the North Pacific, separating it from the Bering Sea. The beautiful Katmai National Park on the northern part of the peninsula contains the awe-inspiring site of the huge 1912 Novarupta Volcano eruption. From here the Aleutian Island Chain, called 'land of the smoky sea,' extends southwest for over a thousand miles. These remote islands, as well as the Pribilof Islands to the north, were the first areas of Alaska discovered by Russia in the eighteenth century.

Russian, Indian and pioneer pasts meld with the present, and civilization and wilderness intertwine in the southwest and southcentral, a region in which all that is Alaska can be found.

Pages 28 & 29: Anchorage, the hub of Alaska, is surrounded by mountains and situated on Cook Inlet on Alaska's gulf coast. The state's center for business and finance, Anchorage is also an emerging world city.
Sunset highlights the beauty of the Matanuska Valley northeast of Anchorage. Settled by drought-stricken Midwest farmers in 1935, this valley now produces half of Alaska's crops.

31

Left: The blanket toss was originally perhaps a means for Eskimo hunters to spot game or to celebrate a successful whale hunt. Here it enlivens festivities at the annual Anchorage Fur Rendezvous in February. Other events include sportscar races on ice, dog sled races, Indian dances and a beard-judging contest.

Above: The World Championship Dog Sled Races during the Anchorage Fur Rendezvous begin and end in the city itself, and run through 25 grueling miles of back country. Many mushers represent communities or villages that have pooled their best dogs and funds to send a competitor to these exciting races.

Right: Farewells are said at the dock where a float plane readies for take-off from the Kenai Peninsula. Bush planes are a practical and common way to travel in Alaska, and provide some of the best sightseeing in remote areas. With most of the state not accessible by road, a large number of Alaskans fly their own planes.

Above: Fishermen in Prince William Sound haul in a hefty catch of salmon. Northeast of the Kenai Peninsula, the Sound offers excellent fishing, which has been a mainstay in the economy of many coastal communities since their beginnings.
Below: Local women of Russian descent work in a fish plant in Homer.
Right: Laying out nets in scenic Prince William Sound.

Right: A contestant tests his skill in the calf-roping competition during the rodeo in Soldotna. Located on the western coast of the Kenai Peninsula, Soldotna sponsors an annual Progress Days celebration in July, which includes the rodeo and a parade.

Below: Sea lions bask on the rocks in Kenai Fjords National Park. Established in 1980 and containing 587,000 acres of glaciers, mountains and steep fjords, the park is a breeding ground for the animals.

Opposite page, top: Two large male Alaskan brown bears fight over a strategic fishing spot in the McNeil River. The McNeil River State Game Sanctuary is located in the northern region of the Alaska Peninsula.

Opposite page, middle left: A brown bear and her cub wander through a valley field. Bears range widely in search of food.

Opposite page, bottom left: A coastal fox curled into napping position rests on a bed of moss near Katmai.

Opposite page, right: A colorful Puffin in the Pribilofs north of the Aleutian chain.

A field of beautiful fireweed blooming in the summer typifies the natural beauty of the Kenai Peninsula.

Left: Lakes, streams and forests enrich the scenic beauty of the mountainous eastern side of the Kenai Peninsula.

Above: A worker on the oil pipeline near Valdez, the southern terminus of the Alaska pipeline which transports oil from Prudhoe Bay on the Arctic shore.

Below: An oil platform in Cook Inlet. The discovery of oil here in the late 1950s caused tremendous growth in the population and economy of the surrounding region.

Opposite page: A graveyard in Eklutna, northeast of Anchorage, reflects the region's cultural history in the Athabaskan Indian spirit house graves topped with Russian Orthodox crosses. In the background is the Old St Nicholas Russian Orthodox log church, built in the mid-1800s.
Left: Boats lie under the winter snow in Bethel. Eighty miles inland from the Bering Sea, the former Eskimo village of Bethel is the largest town in southwestern Alaska.
Above: Located on the north shore of Bristol Bay across from the Alaska Peninsula, the village of Togiak is part of the Togiak National Wildlife Refuge and Wilderness, which extends for more than four million acres.
Below: Lights glow at night in the military housing at Adak in the Aleution Islands, where the United States Navy has a base.

Interior

The great Interior region of Alaska stretches from the Canadian border on the east to about 100 miles from the Bering Sea coast, and from south of the Brooks Range downward to the Alaska Range. The home of the nomadic Athabascan Indians, the Interior was explored by the Russians and the English, and later by Americans, in the nineteenth century. The mighty Yukon River with its many tributaries flows through this land of misty mountains, rolling hills and alpine tundra. The largest mountain in North America at 20,230 feet, Mt McKinley can be seen all the way from Anchorage, 237 miles away, on a clear day. Many roads wind their scenic paths through the Interior and most seem to converge at Fairbanks, the end of the 1520-mile-long Alaska Highway.

The hub of the Interior, Fairbanks is the transportation and supply center for much of the Arctic and the Interior villages and industry. America's northernmost university, the University of Alaska, has its main campus here. Students and professors mingle in Fairbanks, amid log cabins and modern office buildings, with big-game tour guides, prospectors, Indians and military personnel. And although the people of Fairbanks are a mixed lot, they are boisterous and friendly as well.

Like all Alaskan cities, Fairbanks is relatively young. Nothing more than a trading post in 1901, by 1903 the town was beseiged by gold-hungry prospectors hoping to make it big in the nearby gold strike. Although the town's growth from the gold rush eventually ground to a halt, Fairbanks boomed once again in World War II with the Alaska Highway construction, and then again in the 1970s with the discovery of oil in the Arctic and the building of the Alaska pipeline. South of Fairbanks lies the vast Denali National Park and Preserve, its six million acres containing the lofty Mt McKinley. Home to variety of wildlife, including bear, caribou, moose, snowshoe hare, wolves and 130 varieties of birds, the beauty of the park's mountains and tundra, reflected in its many lakes and woven through by glacial streams, typifies the wilderness of Alaska's great Interior.

A partial view of Fairbanks shows the Chena River cutting through the city. With a population of 30,000, Fairbanks is Alaska's second largest community and is considered the heart of the interior.

Pages 44 and 45: An ice fall on Mount McKinley clears a ridge of snow, creating contrasts of light and dark.

Above: Colorful paintings decorate the side of this and many other buildings in Fairbanks, brightening the cityscape during the long, dark winter months, when days can be as short as three hours. Bars such as this offer ample opportunity for natives and visitors to swap tales and songs long into the night.
Right: Tourists board the sternwheeler *Discovery II*, which prepares to embark from Fairbanks on its 4-hour, 25-mile trip up the Chena and Tanana Rivers. One of the sternwheeler's destinations, Cripple Creek, produced $100 million worth of gold during the great rush. An excursion into the past, the boat's trip also takes it by Indian villages and trappers' camps.
Opposite page, top: The trans-Alaska pipeline winds its silvery way through the rolling hills outside of Fairbanks. The pipeline, which was completed in 1977, extends 800 miles and carries one and a half million barrels of oil a day from the Arctic shore to the southern port of Valdez.
Opposite page, bottom: The trans-Alaska pipeline spans the Tanana River near Fairbanks. The 48-inch diameter pipeline continues south over the Alaska Range, over the Chugach Mountains, and through the Keystone Canyon to Valdez. The pipeline runs both above and below ground and has ten pump stations along the way. This massive project triggered a growth in the Alaskan economy and in the population of cities and towns along its route.

An old giant gold dredge at Fox, north of Fairbanks, remains as a relic of past glory. Established before 1905 and named for nearby Fox Creek, the town of Fox was once a busy mining camp.

Left: A dog handler quiets his dogs before the start of the North American Championship Dogsled Races in Fairbanks, held each year in March.
Above: A ptarmigan, Alaska's state bird, wanders through the tundra near Mount McKinley.
Right: An arctic ground squirrel pauses to nibble some food. These squirrels live in communal tunnels under the snow in the winter.
Below: Established in 1917 and expanded in the 1980s, Denali National Park is known for its large numbers of caribou. The caribou gather here in June and migrate to northern summer feeding grounds in July.

Opposite page: The afternoon light and mist create dramatic contrasts in the magnificent Denali National Park. The park's forests are composed of poplar, spruce, aspen and birch.
Right: Mountain climbers scale an ice wall on Mt McKinley. The mountain's highest summit was first reached in 1913.
Above: An Alaska Railroad train comes into the Mt McKinley (now Denali) station. Completed in 1923, the railroad runs between Anchorage and Fairbanks, offering scenic viewing all the way.
Below: Dall sheep graze in a hilly meadow in Denali National Park.

Mt McKinley reflects its rugged beauty in a glacial pond. The mountain's official name, 'Denali,' is the Athabascan Indian name for it and means 'the high one.'

Left: Alpine tundra stretches to the foot of the Alaska Range. Lichens, wildflowers, mosses, small shrubs and other plants with shallow root systems thrive on the tundra, where the permafrost prevents roots from reaching deep into the soil.
Top: A view along ridges and craggy peaks of the Alaska Range, which extends in a 500-mile arc from the Southwest into the Interior and on to the St Elias Mountains. Mt McKinley is part of the Alaska Range.
Above: A field of blue-violet lupines grows in an alpine region near Mt McKinley. Reaching a height of about four feet, these lovely wildflowers are also a common sight along roads or shores

59

Arctic

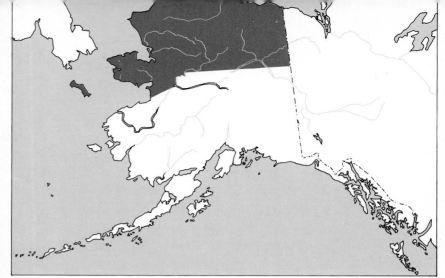

Arctic

From Barrow, the northernmost point on the North American continent, to hospitable Nome, 162 miles east of the Soviet Union, Alaska's Arctic is as intriguing as it is diverse, as extreme as it is untamed. The arctic region of Alaska comprises a third of the state and stretches from the Canadian border to the Bering Sea. With a scant population of 18,000, the Arctic includes 300,000 square miles of land. Although much of the Arctic is rolling tundra, the Brooks Range extends 600 miles east to west. Natural splendor characterizes the huge Gates of the Arctic National Park and Preserve, located in the Brooks Range.

The largest communities in the Arctic have more marked differences than similarities. Located on the southern coast of the Seward Peninsula, Nome has a history steeped in gold rush lore. When gold was discovered in 1898 in nearby Anvil Creek, it didn't take long for the world to harken to its call. In 1899 three million dollars worth of gold was yielded, and by 1903, Nome had exploded into a shantytown with 20,000 inhabitants. Called the 'Gold Rush Capital' of Alaska's northwest, Nome today has a population of about 2800, but its colorful history and lusty living make it a charming and interesting city.

North of Nome and the Arctic Circle, the town of Kotzebue huddles on a sandy peninsula in Kotzebue Sound. The center for commerce and transportation in the northwest Arctic, this town offers a glimpse at native ways of living. The Eskimo population plays a major role also in the character of Barrow, located on the Arctic coast. At 1200 miles from the North Pole, Barrow does not see the sun rise above the horizon for three months in midwinter. In Barrow the past and present coexist in relative peace. But the future is beckoning, and it is beckoning from east of Barrow at Prudhoe Bay. Attention and capital poured into the Arctic with the discovery of oil there in 1968, resulting in higher standards of living as well as increased awareness of the region.

A land of polar bears and reindeer, of oil wells and snowmobiles, of the midnight sun and the northern lights, the Arctic is a unique and compelling frontier.

Located 26 miles north of the Arctic Circle, the town of Kotzebue relies mainly on commercial fishing as well as subsistence hunting.
Pages 60 and 61: Encompassing more than eight million acres astride the Arctic Divide in northcentral Alaska, Gates of the Arctic National Park and Preserve is considered one of the world's finest wilderness areas.

Left: Subtle hues color the sky and a streamlet at midnight in Gates of the Arctic National Park and Preserve on the North slope of the Brooks Range.

Above: Light from an early afternoon sunset bathes this house on Kotzebue Sound. In mid-winter the sun barely rises here for 36 days. The population of Kotzebue is 80 percent Eskimo.

Caribou roam across the tundra north of the Brooks Range, their summer feeding grounds.

Left: An Eskimo woman dries nets and salmon on the banks of the Kobuk River in the northwest. The short Arctic summers are filled with busy preparations for the long and harsh winter months ahead. Dried salmon is put aside for sled dogs; seal and whale meat for people. Although Eskimos work hard in the summer months, in winter they enjoy a more leisurely life. Lovers of sports and music, they engage in community singing and dancing as well as games and contests of skill, such as the high kick or the *muktuk* (whale skin and blubber, an Eskimo delicacy) eating contest.

Above: Eskimos cut up a bowhead whale on the beach at Gambell on St Lawrence Island. Southwest of the Seward Peninsula in the Bering Sea, St Lawrence Island is within sight of Siberia. Gambell, a town on the northwest cape, is a hunting and fishing community. The bowhead whale has long been an Eskimo staple, and a successful whale hunt brings rejoicing as the meat is shared with all. These formidable creatures can weigh more than 70 tons, their jawbones alone measuring 25 feet. Hunting season is in early May.

Above: An Eskimo woman splits a walrus skin, stretched taut on the stretching rack. Walrus skins are used to cover *umiaks*, the long boats used for transportation and for whale hunting. Since the boats must be re-covered every few years and each one takes six skins, these preparations take up most of the late spring. This woman is using an *ulu*, a razor-sharp knife with a curved handle, to do the job.

Left: Two Eskimo women pose at Cape Prince of Wales at the tip of the Seward Peninsula, the westernmost point on the North American continent. The adaptable and practical Eskimos combine old ways and new, as these women's colorful garb indicates. Mail-order items such as down parkas are as popular today as the traditional hand-made *mukluk* footwear.

Right: In addition to providing its inhabitants with a wealth of sea life for subsistence, St Lawrence Island harbors a variety of bird life, including arctic terns, puffins and cormorants. Here an Eskimo woman in Gambell splits walrus hide for umiaks. While the women are busy splitting the hides and sewing them together with sinew thread, the men prepare for the whale hunt by consulting with elders and studying the movements of the ice pack, the weather and the currents.

Left: An Eskimo woman fishes for tom cod in the frozen Unalakleet River.

Right: The rustic charm of Nome is evident in the decor of the Coffee Mine, topped by a polar bear likeness. Destroyed by fire and flood more than once, Nome's unusual appearance is further accentuated by the fact that houses are regularly jacked up or moved to avoid or compensate for permafrost heaves.

Below: Eskimo boys sledding in autumn. In the old days Eskimo children were rarely punished, because, according to ancient belief, the guardian soul of a deceased relative resided in the newborn's body, and the parents could not presume to be wiser than that.

Far right: Tourists try their luck gold-panning in Nome. Although the turn-of-the-century gold rush depleted the readily-available gold, rising gold prices have kindled new interest in ways of extracting the precious metal.

Opposite Top: Since Barrow's population is mainly Eskimo, it is considered the largest Eskimo village in Alaska, with a population of 2800. Although much of the town appears less than charming, with dirt streets and prefabricated houses, Barrow has been recently upgrading itself and has complex research facilities devoted to the study of Arctic ecology. The government's DEW (Distant Early Warning System) started here as well.

Opposite below: A 1:30 am sunrise on pack ice in the Arctic Ocean near Barrow. While the shores at this northern latitude remain frozen in swells and ridges for seven to eight months of the year, break-up signals the start of whale-hunting season.

Right: The crackling cold can practically be seen in this picture of Barrow at −45 degrees. Although winter temperatures average between this and 15 degrees above zero, summer temperatures range in the 40s and the summer sun does not set for 82 days.

Below: A nameless glacier winds its way through the jagged, treeless peaks of the Brooks Range. Extending from the coast to the Canadian border, the mountain range is from 50 to 100 miles wide.

Yukon

Yukon

The very mention of the Yukon brings to mind images of the bonechilling ascent up Chilkoot Pass in the days of the great Klondike Gold Rush. Indeed, the discovery of gold by George Washington Carmacks, Skookum Jim and Tagish Charlie in the summer of 1896 touched off the creation of the Yukon Territory, then a part of the District of Mackenzie. By 1898 the Yukon was its own territory, with a northern border stretching 100 miles along the Beaufort Sea in the Arctic Ocean and a 600-mile-long southern border along the 60th parallel. Alaska lies to the west, the Northwest Territories to the east and British Columbia to the south.

Dawson City, gateway to the gold fields, was named the capital of the Yukon because of its booming population, but over the years its population dwindled to the current figure of less than 1000. The construction of the Alaska Highway during World War II, 600 miles of which run through the Yukon, created a boom for White-horse to the south, which was named the new capital in 1953.

The name Yukon translates as 'big river,' an apt appellation for the Yukon River, which winds 2000 miles from Canada to the Bering Sea. With a sparse population, the Yukon Territory's vast land area is more than twice the size of Great Britain, and much of it remains unspoiled wilderness. Kluane National Park in the southwest typifies the region's beauty—its sparkling lakes, lofty mountains, forested plains and wide valleys comprise a naturalist's paradise. A blanket of wildflowers in the spring, the Yukon tundra takes on the blazing colors of autumn by September. But mountains prevail in much of the territory—and they are some of the steepest in the country—from the St Elias and Coast Mountains in the south, to the Ogilvie and Richardson Mountains northward. Canada's highest peak is found in the Yukon. Glaciers as well as glacial rivers and lakes feed off the mountain snow. And throughout all of the Yukon wildlife abounds, from the Canadian lynx to bear, caribou, smaller mammals and birds.

With its unique and colorful past kept alive in historical landmarks, museums and cities, and with a diverse and breathtaking array of scenic grandeur, the Yukon enriches Canada with the spirit of the wilderness frontier.

An abandoned log cabin and wooden boat lend a ghostly air to scenic Burwash Landing, located on the Alaska Highway and the Kluane Lake in the southwest region of the Yukon Territory.

Pages 76 and 77: Mt Vancouver on the Alaska-Yukon border is part of the St Elias Range. Its jagged peak reaches a height of 15,700 feet.

Left: A Dall ewe and her baby rest on the rocky mountainside. Indigenous to northwestern Canada, Dall sheep live in mountain tundra. Their cloven hooves help them grip mountainous terrain and enable them in winter to dig through the snow to reach edible plants. The growth rings of their horns indicate their age, and their color varies from white to gray and even black.

Right: A grizzly bear pauses on its way across a field. Weighing up to 1000 pounds, grizzly bears vary in color from black to light brown. They are not aggressive animals and are not apt to threaten people unless they are surprised while feeding or are protecting their cubs.

Below: The trees with their autumn foliage along Kathleen Lake in Kluane National Park. Established in 1972, this magnificent park encompasses part of the St Elias Range, including the 19,850-foot-high Mt Logan, Canada's highest peak.

The colorful alpine countryside offers scenic views of mountains and a silvery winding river in Kluane National Park.

Above: In the Yukon's southcentral region east of Whitehorse, the Alaska Highway crosses the Teslin River at Johnson's Crossing. The Teslin River bridge is one of the highway's longest, and was constructed high enough to allow steamers to pass under on their way from Whitehorse.

Right: The Kaskawulsh Glacier pushes itself through the St Elias Mountains.

NOTICES PLACED ON THIS SIGN
WILL BE REMOVED!

THE FAMOUS
WATSON LAKE SIGNPOSTS

IN 1942 A HOMESICK G.I. WORKING ON
THE CONSTRUCTION OF THE ALASKA
HIGHWAY ERECTED A SIGN HERE STATING
THE MILEAGE TO HIS HOME TOWN,
OTHERS FOLLOWED AND TOURISTS STILL
ADD TO THIS COLLECTION.

VILLAGE OF
LAKE ELMO
PERMITS REQUIRED MINN
ORDINANCES ENFORCED

Pages 86 and 87: The famous Watson Lake signpost forest at the north edge of town grows constantly as passing visitors add to the collage. Located in the southeast Yukon, Watson Lake forms the junction of the Alaska and Robert Campbell highways and is the starting point for many sightseers driving through the territory. The town is an important center for distribution, trappers, prospectors, fishermen and the lumber industry.

Above: A dog musher and his weary team on the last leg of the annual Rendezvous Dog Races at Whitehorse. The races are held for three days in February and competition is stiff. Dogs, sleds and mushers fly to Whitehorse from all over the Yukon and Alaska to test their skill and endurance in this exciting event.

Right: Recently restored, Jack London's cabin nestles on wooded grounds in Dawson City. Author of *Call of the Wild, Burning Daylight* and other works that immortalized the wilderness hardships and triumphs of the Klondike quest, Jack London lived in the Yukon and Alaska in 1897 and 1898.

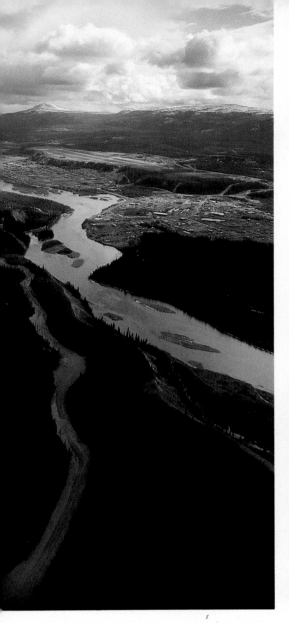

Above left: Whitehorse sprawls along the Yukon River. The territory's capital, Whitehorse, has a population of 17,000— more than two-thirds the population of the entire Yukon. Established in 1900 with the completion of the White Pass & Yukon Route, the city today is the territorial headquarters for the Royal Canadian Mounted Police.

Above: The Palace Grand Theatre in Dawson City was built in 1899 and recently restored. Now a National Historic Site, it features the Gaslight Follies, an old-time variety show for tourists.

Left: A high-kicking chorus line is only one of the features in Whitehorse's Frantic Follies, a hilarious and engaging vaudeville show.

89

Pages 90 and 91: A helicopter perches on a plateau with the majestic peak of Mt Logan rising behind it. The highest peak in Canada, Mt Logan is part of the St Elias Range and can be seen from over 70 miles away. It poses a formidable challenge to mountain-climbing parties.

Above: A rebuilt steamer at Carcross, southeast of Whitehorse, recalls the days of the past, when travel by water was both a necessity and a luxury. The village's name is a shortened version of Caribou Crossing, an appellation given because of the migrating caribou herds that passed through here.

Far right, above: Canoers on the Yukon River pass a derelict sternwheeler partially hidden by trees. Once a crucial link to Dawson City, the sternwheelers brought supplies up the river from Whitehorse, which received the goods by rail from Skagway. With the building of the Alaska Highway and other roads, the sternwheeler became obsolete.

Above right: The *SS Keno* made its last run in 1960 and today this National Historic Site is berthed on the banks of the Yukon River at Dawson City. The role of the riverboat in Dawson's history is an important one, as practically everything had to be brought in, and in a hurry. Goldseekers arrived en masse in the unprepared city in the winter of 1897 and had to wait for supplies until the river thawed in May.

Overleaf, left: A beautiful lake enlivens this wooded valley in the foothills of the Dawson Range.
Overleaf, right: Cross-country skiers enjoy the scenic Auriol Ski Trail in Kluane National Park.
Page 96: The remote mountains in Southwestern Alaska's Katmai area are still black from Mount Katmai's 1912 eruption.

DS
917.98   15143
T

Alaska & the Yukon

DATE DUE